Baritone/Euphonium B.C.—Book 1 **SECOND EDITION**

W61BC

Desktop · Mobile
I P S
INTERACTIVE
Practice Studio
Audio · Video · Extras

Tradition of Excellence™

Comprehensive Band Method

by Bruce Pearson & Ryan Nowlin

Dear Student:

Welcome to your study of the baritone/euphonium—an exciting adventure filled with rewards and challenges. Through careful study and regular practice, you will quickly discover the joy and satisfaction of playing beautiful music for yourself, your family, your friends, or a concert audience. We wish you many rewarding years of baritone/euphonium playing.

Bruce Pearson Bruce Pearson

Ryan Nowlin Ryan Nowlin

PRACTICE JOURNAL

Week	Date Assigned	Assignment/Goal	Minutes Practiced							Total Minutes	Initial
			Su	M	Tu	W	Th	F	Sa		
1											
2											
3											
4											
5											
6											
7											
8											
9											
10											
11											
12											
13											
14											
15											
16											

A full Practice Journal is available from your teacher or from your **INTERACTIVE** Practice Studio.

I P S™
INTERACTIVE
Practice Studio

Enhance your practice by frequently visiting the **INTERACTIVE** Practice Studio. See the inside back cover for more information.

 smartmusic.

Tradition of Excellence is available in SmartMusic. To subscribe, go to www.smartmusic.com.

ISBN 10: 0-8497-7064-5 • ISBN 13: 978-0-8497-7064-7

©2010, 2016 Kjos Music Press, Neil A. Kjos Music Company, Distributor, 4382 Jutland Drive, San Diego, California, 92117.
International copyright secured. All rights reserved. Printed in U.S.A.

Tradition of Excellence and **I P S** INTERACTIVE Practice Studio are trademarks of Kjos Music Press.

For more detailed instruction, be sure to view the Video Lessons in your *Tradition of Excellence* **INTERACTIVE Practice Studio**. Lessons are available every time you see this icon.

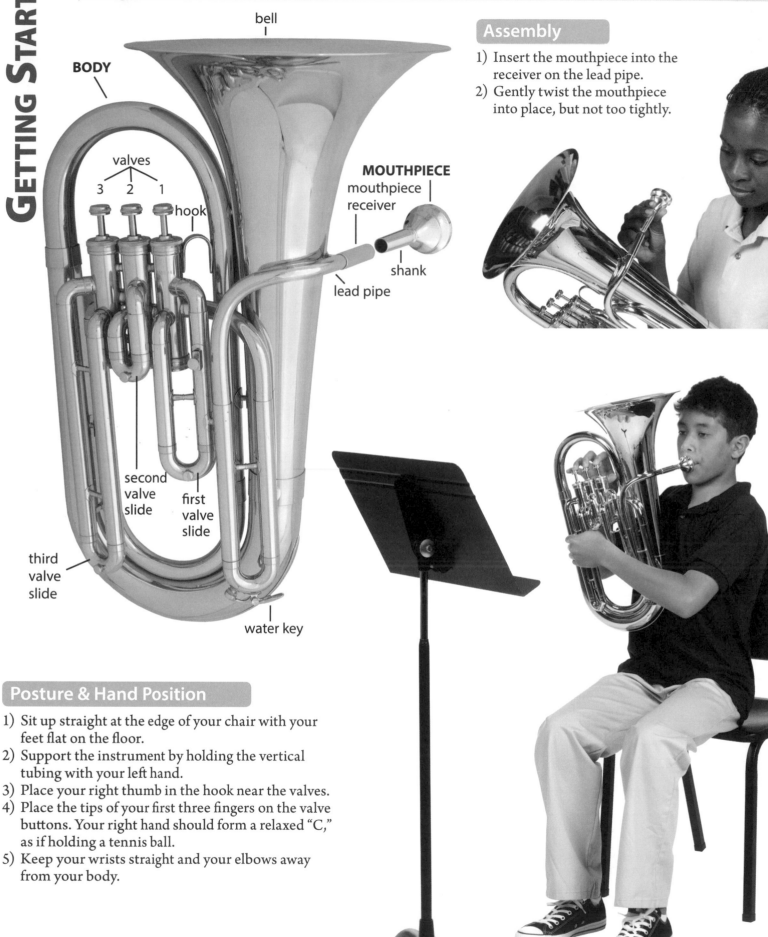

bell

BODY

valves

3 2 1

hook

second valve slide

first valve slide

third valve slide

water key

MOUTHPIECE

mouthpiece receiver

shank

lead pipe

Assembly

1) Insert the mouthpiece into the receiver on the lead pipe.
2) Gently twist the mouthpiece into place, but not too tightly.

Posture & Hand Position

1) Sit up straight at the edge of your chair with your feet flat on the floor.
2) Support the instrument by holding the vertical tubing with your left hand.
3) Place your right thumb in the hook near the valves.
4) Place the tips of your first three fingers on the valve buttons. Your right hand should form a relaxed "C," as if holding a tennis ball.
5) Keep your wrists straight and your elbows away from your body.

Instruments provided courtesy of Conn-Selmer.

Forming an Embouchure & Making a Tone

1) Moisten your lips and shape the inside of your mouth and throat as if you are saying "oh." Bring your lips together as if saying "em."
2) Take a full breath of air through your mouth and blow through closed lips, creating a relaxed buzz.

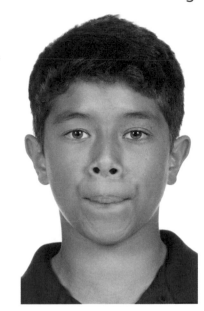

3) Remove the mouthpiece from the instrument and hold it by the shank. Without using too much pressure, place the mouthpiece over the center of the buzz with equal amounts of the mouthpiece on the upper and lower lip. Use a mirror to check your embouchure.
4) Take a full breath of air through your mouth and play a long, steady buzz.
5) Complete the **Mouthpiece Workout** by watching the video lesson and playing along with the recorded accompaniment (see the inside back cover for details).

Daily Care & Maintenance

Putting the Baritone/Euphonium Away

1) Depress the water key and blow (not buzz) through the instrument to empty excess water.
2) Wipe off the instrument with a soft, clean cloth.
3) Push in all slides, making sure you depress the corresponding valve when moving a slide.
4) Remove the mouthpiece and place it and the instrument in the case. Latch the case.

Oiling the Valves (Daily)

1) Gently remove only the first valve by unscrewing it at the top of the valve casing (not the valve button). Do not turn the valve or touch any part that is protected by the casing.
2) Apply 5 or 6 drops of valve oil along the metal part of the valve in which there are holes.
3) Carefully insert the valve back into the baritone/euphonium, aligning the valve guide with the corresponding groove in the valve casing, and screw in the valve at the top of the valve casing.
4) Push the valve button up and down rapidly to work in the valve oil.
5) Repeat this process with the other valves.

Greasing the Slides (Regularly)

1) To remove the slide, depress the corresponding valve button and pull out the slide. (For the main tuning slide, there is no need to depress any valves.) Only remove one slide at a time.
2) Remove existing grease by wiping the slide with a rag.
3) Apply a generous amount of grease to the slide.
4) Insert the slide back into the baritone/euphonium.
5) Keeping the valve depressed, move the slide in and out of the instrument to work in the grease.
6) Push the slide all the way in and wipe off the excess grease with a rag.
7) Return the slide to its original position and repeat with the other slides.

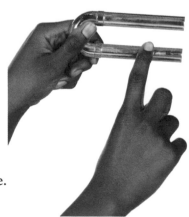

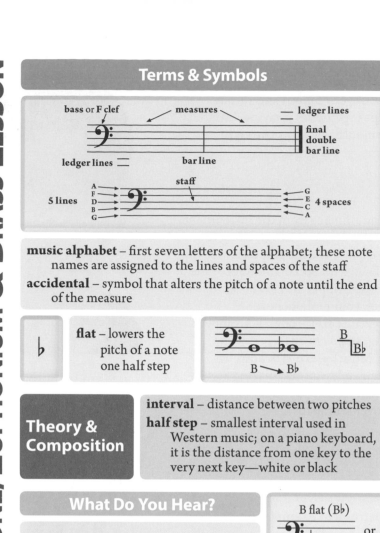

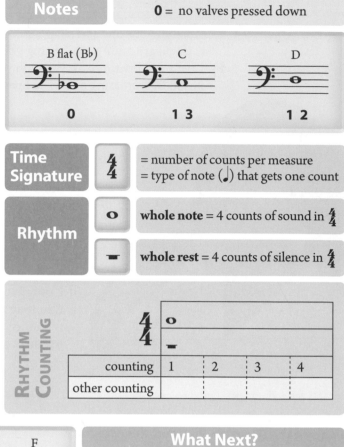

BARITONE/EUPHONIUM & BRASS LESSON

Terms & Symbols

Notes

0 = no valves pressed down

music alphabet – first seven letters of the alphabet; these note names are assigned to the lines and spaces of the staff

accidental – symbol that alters the pitch of a note until the end of the measure

flat – lowers the pitch of a note one half step

B → B♭

Theory & Composition

interval – distance between two pitches

half step – smallest interval used in Western music; on a piano keyboard, it is the distance from one key to the very next key—white or black

Time Signature

4/4 = number of counts per measure = type of note (♩) that gets one count

Rhythm

o whole note = 4 counts of sound in 4/4

– whole rest = 4 counts of silence in 4/4

RHYTHM COUNTING

4/4	o			
	–			
counting	1	2	3	4
other counting				

What Do You Hear?

When you play your instrument, you will probably play one of these two notes:

B flat (B♭) 0 or F 0

What Next?

Ask your teacher which note you are playing: If your natural note is B♭, start on page 4. If your natural note is F, start on page 5.

Use the audio, video, and extras provided in your *Tradition of Excellence* **INTERACTIVE Practice Studio** to enhance every practice session. See the inside back cover for more information.

staff & bar lines, accidental, ♭

1. The First Note ▸ How is your posture?

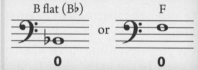

2. The Second Note ▸ Are you using plenty of air?

3. Music in Motion ▸ Are you playing with a good embouchure?

4. All Together, Now! ▸ How is your hand position?

5. Mr. Whole Note Takes a Walk ▸ Write the note names beneath the music before you play.

BARITONE/EUPHONIUM & BRASS LESSON

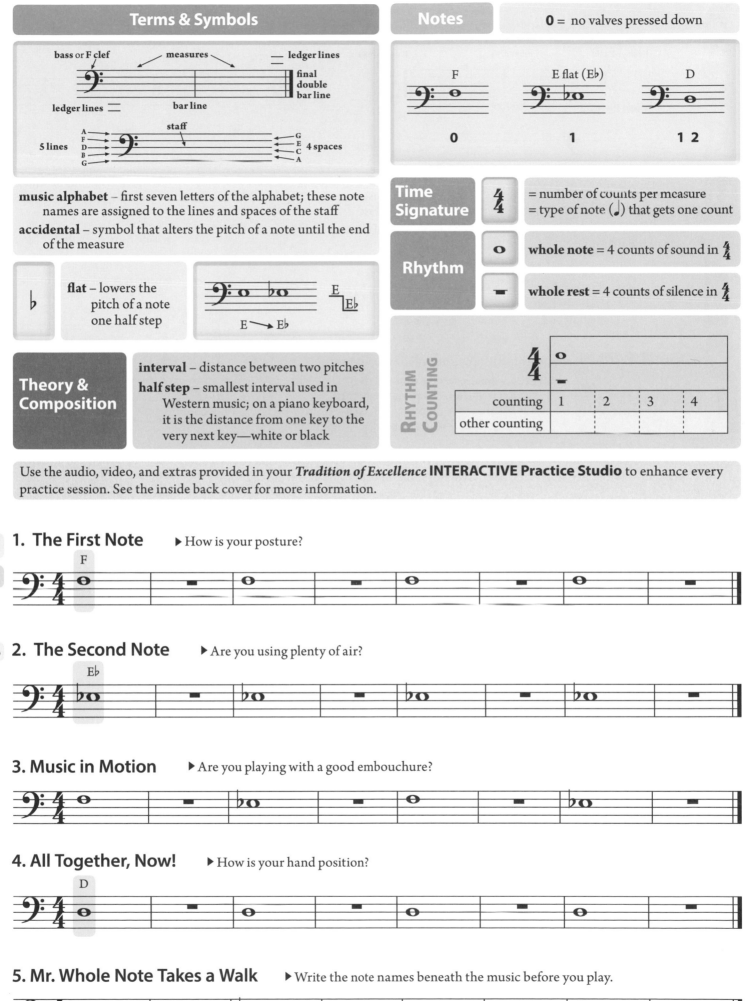

Terms & Symbols

bass or F clef
measures
ledger lines
final double bar line
ledger lines
bar line
staff
5 lines
A F D B G
G E C A
4 spaces

music alphabet – first seven letters of the alphabet; these note names are assigned to the lines and spaces of the staff

accidental – symbol that alters the pitch of a note until the end of the measure

flat – lowers the pitch of a note one half step

E → E♭

Theory & Composition

interval – distance between two pitches

half step – smallest interval used in Western music; on a piano keyboard, it is the distance from one key to the very next key—white or black

Notes

0 = no valves pressed down

F	E flat (E♭)	D
0	1	1 2

Time Signature

4/4 = number of counts per measure
= type of note (♩) that gets one count

Rhythm

𝅝 **whole note** = 4 counts of sound in 4/4

▬ **whole rest** = 4 counts of silence in 4/4

RHYTHM COUNTING

counting	1	2	3	4
other counting				

Use the audio, video, and extras provided in your *Tradition of Excellence* **INTERACTIVE Practice Studio** to enhance every practice session. See the inside back cover for more information.

staff & bar lines

1. The First Note
▶ How is your posture?

F

2. The Second Note
▶ Are you using plenty of air?

accidental, ♭

E♭

3. Music in Motion
▶ Are you playing with a good embouchure?

4. All Together, Now!
▶ How is your hand position?

D

5. Mr. Whole Note Takes a Walk
▶ Write the note names beneath the music before you play.

FULL BAND

Terms & Symbols

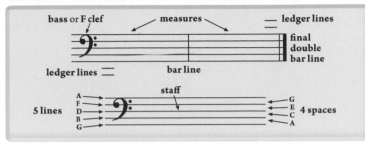

bass or F clef — measures — ledger lines
final double bar line
ledger lines — bar line
staff
5 lines — 4 spaces

music alphabet – first seven letters of the alphabet; these note names are assigned to the lines and spaces of the staff

accidental – symbol that alters the pitch of a note until the end of the measure

flat – lowers the pitch of a note one half step

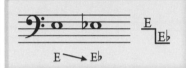

E → Eb

Theory & Composition

interval – distance between two pitches

half step – smallest interval used in Western music; on a piano keyboard, it is the distance from one key to the very next key—white or black

Notes

0 = no valves pressed down

D — 1 2
E flat (Eb) — 1
F — 0

Time Signature

4/4 = number of counts per measure
= type of note (♩) that gets one count

Rhythm

○ **whole note** = 4 counts of sound in 4/4

▬ **whole rest** = 4 counts of silence in 4/4

COUNTING & CONDUCTING

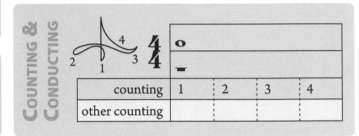

	counting	1	2	3	4
	other counting				

Use the audio, video, and extras provided in your *Tradition of Excellence* **INTERACTIVE Practice Studio** to enhance every practice session. See the inside back cover for more information.

---

staff & bar lines

4/4 ○ ▬

1. Away We Go!   ▶ How is your posture?

D

---

accidental, ♭

2. Going Up?   ▶ Are you playing with a steady air stream to produce a smooth, even sound?

Eb

---

3. Count Me In   ▶ 1) Write the counting under the music. 2) Clap the rhythm.
3) Sing the notes using "too," the note names, or solfège. 4) Play!

---

4. Higher Ground   ▶ Are you playing with a good embouchure?

F

---

5. Moving Around   TEST   ▶ Write the note names beneath the music before you play.

---

6. Baritone/Euphonium Private Lesson

▶ Here is how to draw a bass clef.
  1)   2)

▶ Draw eight bass clefs on your own. Be sure to draw the dots on both sides of the fourth (F) line.

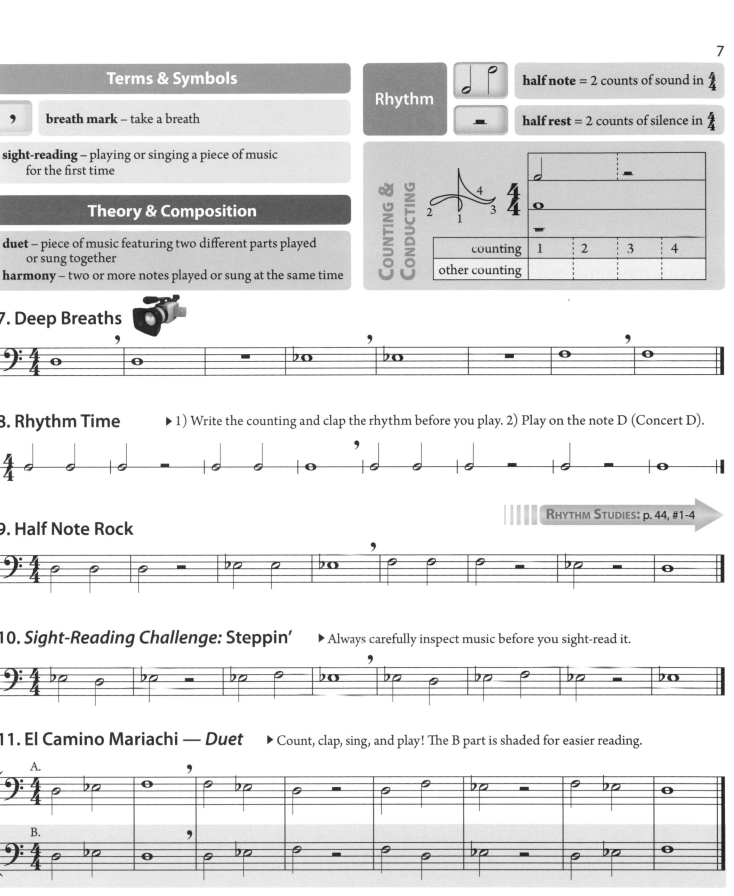

Terms & Symbols

, **breath mark** – take a breath

sight-reading – playing or singing a piece of music for the first time

Theory & Composition

duet – piece of music featuring two different parts played or sung together

harmony – two or more notes played or sung at the same time

Rhythm

half note = 2 counts of sound in 4/4

half rest = 2 counts of silence in 4/4

COUNTING & CONDUCTING

counting	1	2	3	4
other counting				

7. Deep Breaths

8. Rhythm Time

▶ 1) Write the counting and clap the rhythm before you play. 2) Play on the note D (Concert D).

9. Half Note Rock

RHYTHM STUDIES: p. 44, #1-4

10. *Sight-Reading Challenge:* Steppin'

▶ Always carefully inspect music before you sight-read it.

11. El Camino Mariachi — *Duet*

▶ Count, clap, sing, and play! The B part is shaded for easier reading.

A.

B.

12. Cuckoo ✓ TEST

Traditional

13. Excellence in Ear Training

▶ Practice with the recorded accompaniment. Listen in measures 1, 3, 5, and 7. In measures 2, 4, 6, and 8, echo what you heard. Your starting notes are shown.

1 Listen 2 Play 3 Listen 4 Play 5 Listen 6 Play 7 Listen 8 Play

W61BC

Rhythm

quarter note = 1 count of sound in $\frac{4}{4}$

quarter rest = 1 count of silence in $\frac{4}{4}$

COUNTING & CONDUCTING

| counting | 1 | 2 | 3 | 4 |
| other counting | | | | |

Notes

C   B flat (B♭)

1 3   0

14. Rhythm Time ▸ 1) Write the counting and clap the rhythm before you play. 2) Play on the note D (Concert D).

RHYTHM STUDIES: p. 44, #5-17

15. Rising Rhythms ▸ Start each note by whispering the word "too."

16. Stepping Stones ▸ Keep the air moving.

17. Rain, Rain   Traditional

18. In a Minor Mood ▸ Count, clap, sing, and play!

19. Hot Cross Buns ▸ When playing low notes, keep the inside of your mouth open and your teeth apart.   English Folk Song

20. Go Tell Aunt Rhodie ✓ TEST   American Folk Song

21. Baritone/Euphonium Private Lesson ▸ 1) Draw a bass clef at the beginning of the staff.
2) Trace the notes, accidental, and rests, and draw three more of each.

Terms & Symbols

Solo – only one person plays or sings
Soli – a small group or section plays or sings
Tutti – everyone plays or sings

repeat sign – play or sing the music again

Time Signature

C common time = $\frac{4}{4}$

Theory & Composition

phrase – musical sentence, often 4 or 8 measures long
round – song in which the same part is played or sung by two or more groups starting at different times
composition – creation of music that can be performed later, usually from written notation

Solo, Tutti
phrase

22. Little Robin Redbreast
Traditional

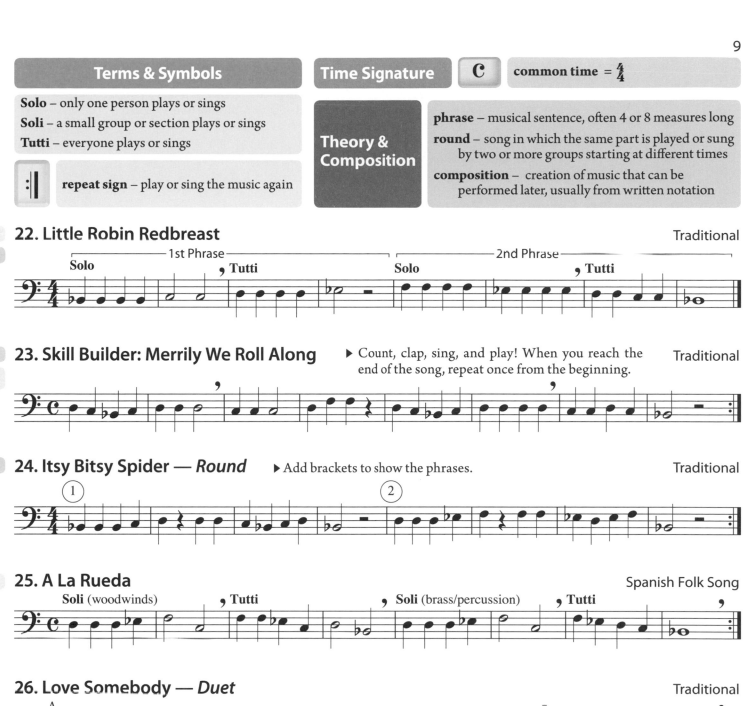

23. Skill Builder: Merrily We Roll Along
▶ Count, clap, sing, and play! When you reach the end of the song, repeat once from the beginning.
Traditional

c

24. Itsy Bitsy Spider — *Round*
▶ Add brackets to show the phrases.
Traditional

round

25. A La Rueda
Spanish Folk Song

Soli

26. Love Somebody — *Duet*
Traditional

27. Good King Wenceslas ✔ TEST
Traditional English Carol

28. Excellence in Composition
▶ 1) Draw a bass clef. 2) Complete and play your composition.

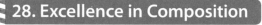

Title _____ Composer _____

Terms & Symbols	**articulation** – type of attack used to play a note or group of notes		**slur** – articulation that connects notes of *different* pitches; indicates a very smooth sound with only the first note tongued	Notes
		one-measure repeat sign – play or sing the previous measure again		G 1 2

slur

29. Warm-up: Serenity — *Round*   ▶ Keep the air moving.

30. Chop Builder   ▶ Make a clean slur from D to G.

31. Camptown Races

▶ Draw the missing notes in the ovals before you play.

Stephen Foster, America's first great popular songwriter, was born on the 50th anniversary of American Independence: the Fourth of July, 1826.

Stephen Foster (1826–1864) American Composer

Solo/Soli   Tutti   Solo/Soli   Tutti

32. Skill Builder   ▶ Add brackets to show the phrases.

33. London Bridge — *Duet*   English Folk Song

A.

B.

34. The Frog's Song — *Round*   ✔ TEST   ▶ Are you slurring?   Japanese Folk Song

35. Baritone/Euphonium Private Lesson

▶ Play with a fast and steady air stream.

▶ Repeat this exercise using the following fingerings: 0, 2, 1, 12, 23, 13, 123. Use this as a daily warm-up when you practice. Also play this exercise on your mouthpiece.

MASTERING EXCELLENCE: p. 38, #1

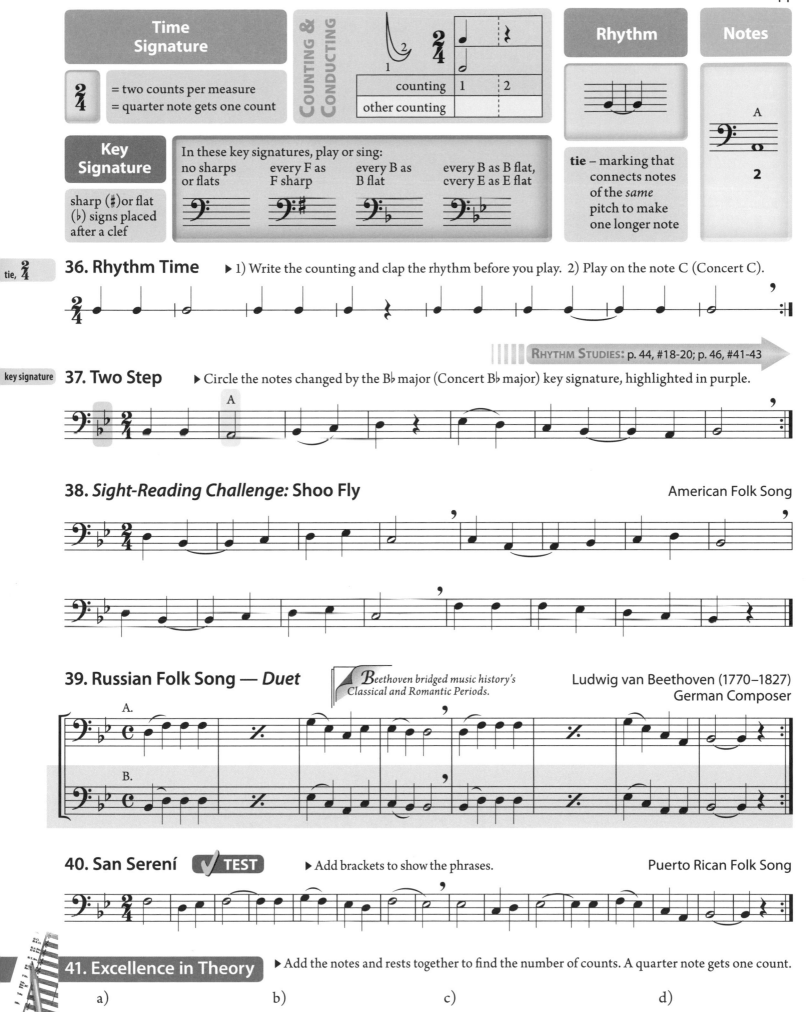

Theory & Composition	**Terms & Symbols**
trio – piece of music featuring three different parts played or sung together	 **rehearsal numbers** – find important places in the music using these markers
introduction – opening passage of a piece of music	**1st and 2nd endings** – play or sing the 1st ending the first time through, repeat, skip the 1st ending, and play or sing the 2nd ending the second time through
theme – a melody within a piece of music	**fermata** – hold a note or rest longer than its usual value

Concert Etiquette

—Enter the stage or performance area confidently. Make eye contact with the audience and smile.
—Stand or sit tall. Be positive and energetic. It's fun to share your music with others!

trio, introduction, theme

rehearsal numbers, 1st & 2nd endings

Solo: A   **Duet:** A + B   **Trio** or **Full Band:** A + B + C

Jingle Bells

J.S. Pierpont (1822–1893)
American Composer

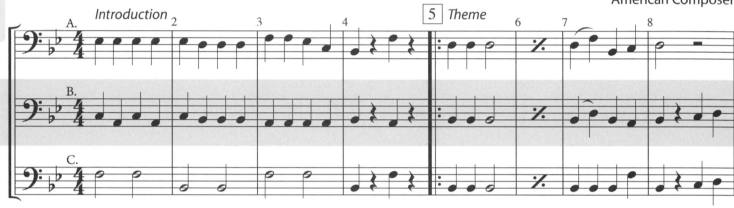

▶ Repeat back to 5 .

Jolly Old St. Nicholas

Traditional

The Dreidel Song

Jewish Folk Song

Kwanzaa Celebration

David Bobrowitz (b. 1945)
American Composer

Rhythm

eighth note = ½ count of sound in **2/4**, **4/4**, or **C**

a single eighth note has a **flag**

a group of eighth notes is connected by a **beam**

COUNTING & CONDUCTING

	counting	1 &	2 &	3 &	4 &
	other counting				

42. Warm-up: Breath Support Challenge ▶ Take a deep breath and play with your best tone while holding the pitch for as long as you can. On which beat did you finish?

1 2 3 4   5 6 7 8   9 10 11 12   13 14 15 16   17 18 19 20   21 22 23 24   25 26 27 28   29 30 31 32

43. Epic Eighth Notes ▶ The bottom line provides the basic pulse.

Clap

44. Michael Finnegan ▶ Count, clap, sing, and play!   Irish Folk Song

1.   2.

45. Eighth Note Escapade

Clap

46. Skill Builder: Processional Dance ▶ Count, clap, sing, and play!   Renaissance Dance Music

1.   2.

47. Baja Breeze ✓ TEST

1.   2.

48. Baritone/Euphonium Private Lesson ▶ 1) Write the note names. 2) Fill in the fingering for each note.

D   1 2

Theory & Composition | **improvisation** – spontaneous composition of music through playing or singing

49. Unforgettable Eighth Notes

50. Mahnomen Harvest ▶ Count, clap, sing, and play!

51. Eighth Notes on the Edge

52. Now Let Me Fly ▶ Count, clap, sing, and play!

Spirituals are religious folk songs created in the 18th and 19th centuries.

American Spiritual

53. *Sight-Reading Challenge:* Promenade ▶ 1) Write the counting and draw the bar lines. 2) Sight-read!

54. Rio Con Brio ✔ TEST

55. Excellence in Improvisation ▶ Play along with the recorded accompaniment. Measures 1-2: Play the written notes. Measures 3-5: Improvise using the same notes.

Rhythm

pick-up or **anacrusis** – music that comes before the first full measure; rhythmic value of the pick-up is sometimes removed from the last measure

Notes

A flat (A♭)

1

Key Signature

E♭ major (Concert E♭ major) – play or sing every B as B♭, E as E♭, A as A♭

Theory & Composition

theme and variation – type of composition that begins with a main melody (**theme**) and continues with different versions (**variations**) of the main melody

56. Warm-up: Chorale — *Duet*

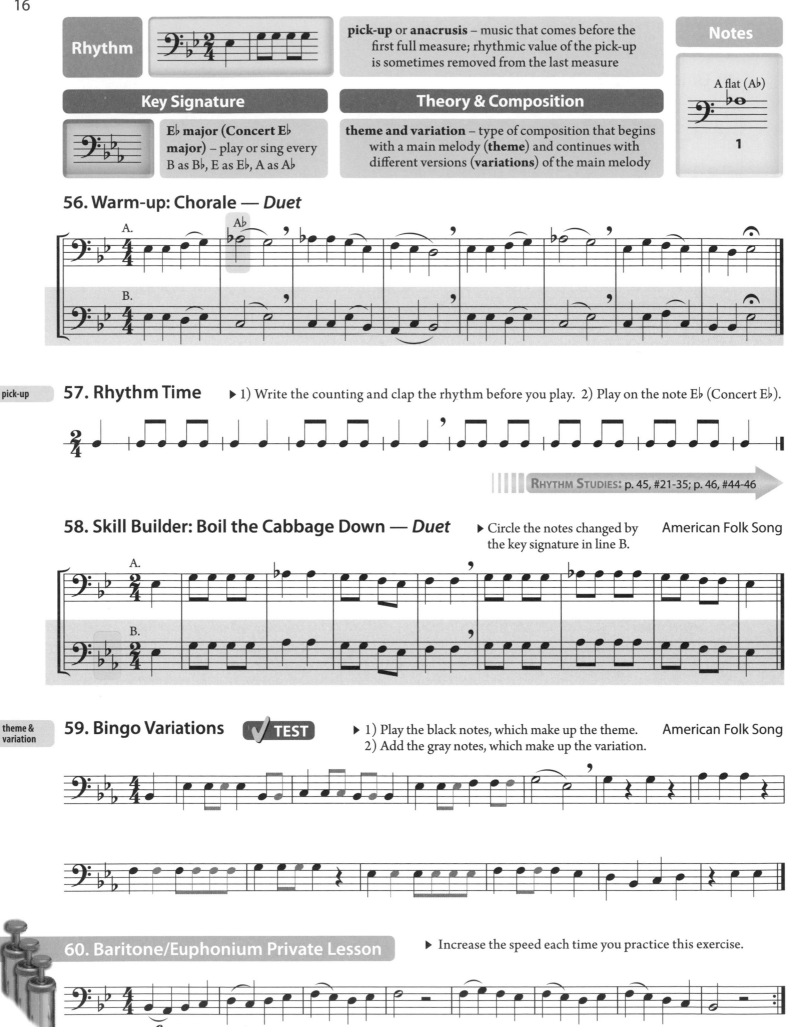

pick-up

57. Rhythm Time
▶ 1) Write the counting and clap the rhythm before you play. 2) Play on the note E♭ (Concert E♭).

RHYTHM STUDIES: p. 45, #21-35; p. 46, #44-46

58. Skill Builder: Boil the Cabbage Down — *Duet*
▶ Circle the notes changed by the key signature in line B.

American Folk Song

theme & variation

59. Bingo Variations
✓ **TEST**
▶ 1) Play the black notes, which make up the theme.
2) Add the gray notes, which make up the variation.

American Folk Song

60. Baritone/Euphonium Private Lesson
▶ Increase the speed each time you practice this exercise.

mf

MASTERING EXCELLENCE: p. 38, #2

Rhythm · **dot** – adds half the value of the note

♩. = ♩ ♩ = ♩.
2 + 1 = 2 + 1 = 3

dotted half note = 3 counts of sound in ¾, 4/4, or 𝄵

Time Signature ¾ = three counts per measure = quarter note gets one count

COUNTING & CONDUCTING

	counting	1 &	2 &	3 &
	other counting			

Terms & Symbols

dynamics – softness or loudness of a piece of music

p **piano** – soft

f **forte** – loud

61. Rhythm Time ▶ 1) Write the counting and clap the rhythm before you play. 2) Play on the note E♭ (Concert E♭).

RHYTHM STUDIES: p. 46, #49-53

62. Encounter in Three ▶ Circle the notes changed by the key signature.

63. Skill Builder: A Simple Waltz

p

64. *Sight-Reading Challenge:* **Theme from "Cambridge Overture"**

Anne McGinty is one of the most prolific female composers of band music and has over 225 pieces published for band, orchestra, and flute.

Anne McGinty (b. 1945) American Composer

f

From *Cambridge Overture* (Q881077), ©1991 Edmondson & McGinty. All rights assigned Queenwood/Kjos 2002. Used with permission.

65. I've Just Come From Sydney ✓ **TEST**

Australian Folk Song

p *f*

66. Excellence in Composition: Carnival of Venice

Italian Folk Song

▶ 1) Play the theme. 2) Add eighth notes after some of the quarter notes to compose a variation as in **59. Bingo Variations**. **Bonus:** Improvise a variation!

f

| Terms & Symbols | tempo – speed of a piece of music
Andante – walking tempo; slower than **Moderato**
Moderato – medium tempo
Allegro – fast tempo | *mp*
mf | *mezzo piano* – medium soft
mezzo forte – medium loud | accent – emphasize the note |

Andante

67. Warm-up: Lullaby
▶ Use plenty of air to sustain each pitch.
Welsh Folk Song

Andante

Allegro

68. Ezekiel Saw the Wheel — *Duet*
American Spiritual

Allegro

mp, >
Moderato

69. Rhythm Time
▶ 1) Write the counting and clap the rhythm before you play. 2) Play on the note B♭ (Concert B♭).

Moderato

RHYTHM STUDIES: p. 46, #54-58

70. *Sight-Reading Challenge:* Streets of Laredo
Laredo is a city in Texas on the Mexican border. American Folk Song

Moderato

mf

71. Skill Builder: Donkey Riding
▶ 1) Add brackets to show the phrases.
2) Add a breath mark between the phrases.
Canadian Folk Song

Moderato

72. Theme from "The Nutcracker" ✓TEST
Tchaikovsky first studied to be a lawyer but eventually became a full-time composer thanks to the support of a wealthy patron.
Peter Ilyich Tchaikovsky (1840–1893)
Russian Composer

Andante

73. Baritone/Euphonium Private Lesson
▶ Increase the tempo slightly each time you practice this exercise. Learning these fingering patterns is important to your progress.

MASTERING EXCELLENCE: p. 38, #3

Solo

As a soloist, at the end of your performance, bow to acknowledge the applause of the audience, then gratefully gesture towards your accompanist so that he or she may also receive recognition from the audience.

The Good Life
Solo with Piano Accompaniment

Ryan Nowlin (b. 1978)
American Composer

In addition to his work as a composer and author, Ryan Nowlin is a music teacher, horn player, and singer.

BAND PIECES

Theory & Composition	Terms & Symbols
chord – two or more notes sounded at the same time	**long rest** or **multiple-measure rest** – rest for the number of measures indicated
closing – last measures of a composition, often containing music added to give a feeling of finality	

Concert Etiquette

—If you make a mistake, never let it show. Keep playing or singing as if nothing happened.
—When you are finished, graciously accept the audience's applause. Leave the stage area confidently.

chord

Warm-up: Tone, Balance, and Tuning

▶ There are many ways to perform a warm-up; follow the instructions given by your director.

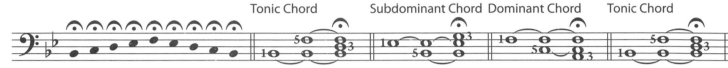

Tonic Chord   Subdominant Chord Dominant Chord   Tonic Chord

closing

March Across the Seas

Bruce Pearson played clarinet and saxophone as well as baseball and hockey into his college years before becoming a music teacher, author, composer, and conductor.

Bruce Pearson (b. 1942) and
Ryan Nowlin (b. 1978)
American Composers

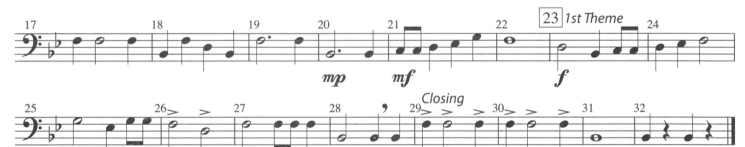

Procession
from "Water Music"

Water Music was written for a royal boat party on England's Thames River. The orchestra played from one barge while King George I and friends listened from another vessel close by.

George Frideric Handel (1685–1759)
English Composer
arr. Ryan Nowlin

long rest

▶ In ²/₄, ³/₄, and other time signatures, ▬ indicates a full measure of rest.

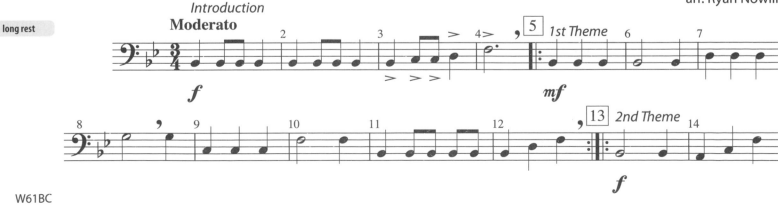

Banana Boat Song

Jamaican Folk Song
arr. Ryan Nowlin

Indigo Rock

Bruce Pearson & Ryan Nowlin
American Composers

Terms & Symbols

crescendo – gradually louder
decrescendo – gradually softer

natural – cancels a flat (♭) or sharp (♯)

Notes

A flat (A♭)

1

divisi (div.) – some performers play or sing the top notes while others play or sing the bottom notes
unisono (unis.) – everyone plays or sings the same notes

74. Warm-up: "Werde munter" — Duet

Johann Schop was a virtuoso violinist but also played cornet and trombone. This melody by Schop was used by J.S. Bach in his famous Cantata 147.

Johann Schop (1590–1667)
German Composer

75. Fais Dodo

▸ For low notes, keep the inside of your mouth open with your teeth apart.

French Folk Song

76. Baroque March

Though considered an English composer, Handel was born in Germany.

George Frideric Handel (1685–1759)
English Composer

77. La Bamba

▸ Circle the notes changed by the key signature.

Mexican Folk Song

divisi, unisono, ♮

78. Skill Builder   ✔ TEST

79. Baritone/Euphonium Private Lesson

▸ Also play this exercise on your mouthpiece alone.

MASTERING EXCELLENCE: p. 38, #4

Theory & Composition

whole step – interval consisting of two half steps
major scale – series of whole (w) and half (h) steps
in the following pattern: 1 2 3 4 5 6 7 8
w w h w w w h
arpeggio – notes of a chord sounded one after another
orchestration – choice of instruments used to play the music

Notes

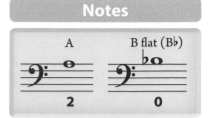

80. Going Up or Down?

Andante

81. Just By Accident

Andante

82. *Sight-Reading Challenge:*
Theme from "Orpheus In the Underworld"

In addition to composing, Jacques Offenbach was a fine cellist.

Jacques Offenbach (1819–1880)
French Composer

Allegro

major scale, arpeggio

83. B♭ Major Scale, Arpeggio, and Chords (Concert B♭ Major)

Major Scale   Arpeggio   Chords

orchestration

84. Crescent Moon Rising

Andante

Chinese Folk Song

Orchestration: Full Band ———————   Woodwinds & Percussion———   Brass & Percussion ———   Full Band ———————

85. Skill Builder ✔ TEST   ▶ Also play with other articulations: A) B) C)

Moderato

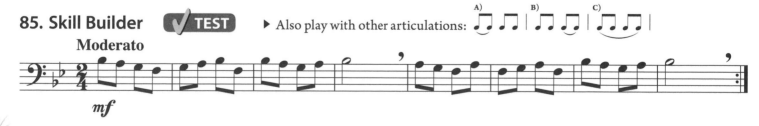

86. Excellence in Improvisation

▶ Play along with the recorded accompaniment. Measures 1-2: Play the written notes.

Measures 3-5: Improvise using

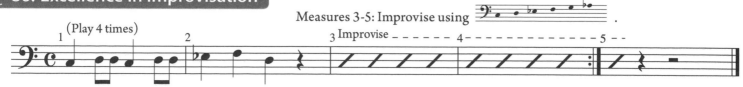

W61BC

Terms & Symbols	Key Signature	Notes

**sharp** – raises the pitch of a note one half step

F → F#

(b)   **courtesy accidental** or **cautionary accidental** – reminder that the bar line has canceled an accidental

F major (Concert F major) – play or sing every B as Bb

E   F sharp (F#)

2   2 3

87. Warm-up: Chop Builders
▶ Also play this exercise on your mouthpiece alone.

Andante

88. Song of Remembrance
Moderato

89. F Major Scale, Arpeggio, and Chords (Concert F Major)
Major Scale   Arpeggio   Chords

90. Santa Lucia
▶ Circle the notes changed by the key signature. Also circle every E♮.

Italian Folk Song

Moderato

courtesy accidental

91. *Sight-Reading Challenge:* Boogie Blues
Allegro

div.

92. Skill Builder ✓TEST
Moderato

93. Baritone/Euphonium Private Lesson

▶ Repeat Exercise A using the following fingerings: 0, 2, 1, 12, 23, 13, 123. Use this as a daily warm-up when you practice. Also play this exercise on your mouthpiece alone.

A

B

F#

MASTERING EXCELLENCE: p. 39, #5

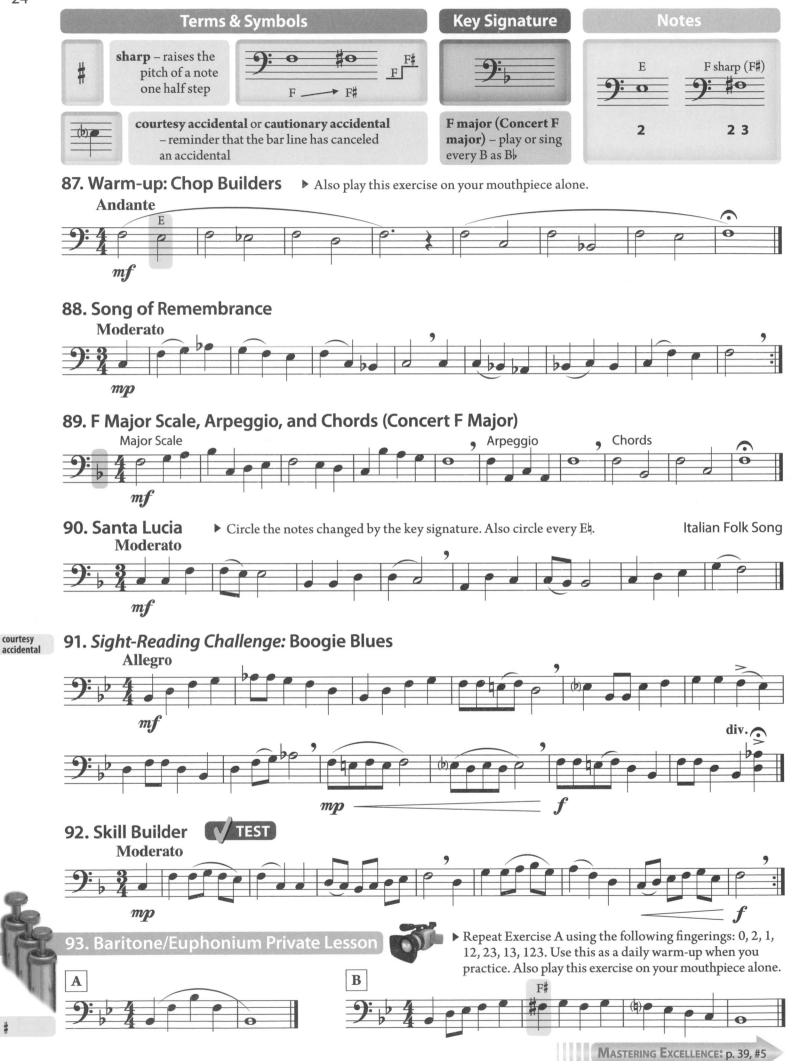

Terms & Symbols — staccato – shorten the note

94. Warm-up: Tone Builder
Andante

95. E♭ Major Scale, Arpeggio, and Chords (Concert E♭ Major)
Major Scale — Arpeggio — Chords

96. When the Saints Go Marching In
When the Saints Go Marching In is often performed in a Dixieland jazz style. Dixieland originated in New Orleans, Louisiana in the early 20th century.
American Spiritual
Allegro

staccato

97. Musette
Bach's death marked the end of the Baroque Period.
Johann Sebastian Bach (1685–1750)
German Composer
Allegro — Solo/Soli — Tutti

98. Bella Bimba
Italian Folk Song
Moderato

99. Skill Builder ✓ TEST
Moderato

100. Excellence in Ear Training
▶ Practice with the recorded accompaniment. Listen in measures 1, 3, 5, and 7. In measures 2, 4, 6, and 8, echo what you heard. Your starting notes are shown.

1 Listen · 2 Play · 3 Listen · 4 Play · 5 Listen · 6 Play · 7 Listen · 8 Play

Rhythm ♩. ♪.

dotted quarter note = 1½ counts of sound in ²⁄₄, ³⁄₄, ⁴⁄₄, or **C**

COUNTING & CONDUCTING

	counting	1	&	2	&
	other counting				

Terms & Symbols

Da Capo al Fine (D.C. al Fine) – go back to the beginning of the piece and play or sing until the *Fine*

101. Warm-up: Chop Builders
▶ Play with a fast, steady air stream. Also play this exercise on your mouthpiece alone.
Andante

102. Low Down
Andante

103. Dotted Quarters
▶ The bottom line provides the basic pulse.
Moderato

Clap

RHYTHM STUDIES: p. 45, #36–40; p. 46, #47–48, 59–60

D.C. al Fine

104. Alouette
▶ Orchestrate by writing in the instruments that will play each four-measure section.

French Canadian Folk Song

Allegro *Fine*

Orchestration: _____

D.C. al Fine

105. Ronde   ✓ TEST
Moderato

Tielman Susato was a Renaissance composer, trumpet player, and music publisher. He wrote mostly dance music, including Ronde.

Tielman Susato (c. 1500–c. 1562)
Flemish (Belgian) Composer

106. Baritone/Euphonium Private Lesson
▶ Increase tempo slightly each time you practice this exercise.
Learning these fingering patterns is important to your progress.

MASTERING EXCELLENCE: p. 39, #6

Terms & Symbols | **Maestoso** – majestically

107. Soar!

Andante

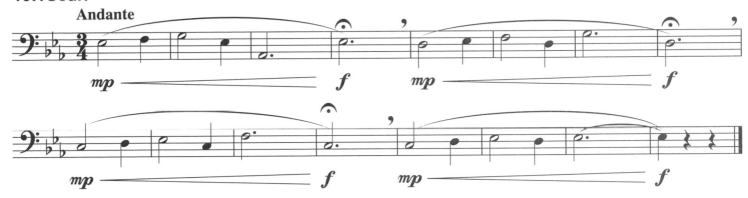

108. Skill Builder

Moderato

109. *Sight-Reading Challenge:* Theme from "The Red Balloon"

Anne McGinty (b. 1945)
American Composer

Moderato

From *The Red Balloon* (Q882119), ©1993 Edmondson & McGinty. All rights assigned Queenwood/Kjos 2002. Used with permission.

Maestoso

110. Trumpet Voluntary — *Duet* ✓TEST

Trumpet Voluntary is also known as *Prince of Denmark's March* and was originally composed for harpsichord.

Jeremiah Clarke
(c. 1674–1707)
English Composer

Introduction
Maestoso

111. Excellence in Theory

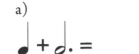

▶ Add the notes and rests together to find the number of counts. A quarter note gets one count.

a) ♩ + ♩. = ___   b) ♪ + 𝄽 = ___   c) ♩. + ♩ + ♫ = ___   d) 𝄽 + ♪ + ♩. = ___

112. Warm-up: Range, Tone, and Tuning
▶ Also play this exercise on your mouthpiece alone.

Andante

113. Skill Builder
Moderato

114. Look Before You Leap
Andante

115. In the Bleak Midwinter — *Duet*

20th Century composer Gustav Holst was a professional trombonist. In the Bleak Midwinter was originally written for congregational singing.

Gustav Holst (1874–1934)
English Composer

Andante

A.

B.

116. Theme from "Symphony No. 9" ✓ TEST

Beethoven was completely deaf when he wrote Symphony No. 9 in 1824.

Ludwig van Beethoven
(1770–1827)
German Composer

Moderato

117. Baritone/Euphonium Private Lesson
▶ 1) Write the note names. 2) Fill in the fingerings for each note.

Erin Watson was born in Wichita Falls, Texas, the Lone Star State. She plays violin, piano, and accordion. She studied with famed American composer Joan Tower.

118. Lone Star Waltz

▶ 1) Orchestrate by writing in the instruments that will play each two-measure section of the music. 2) Add dynamics.

Erin A. Watson (b. 1977)
American Composer

Andante

119. *Sight-Reading Challenge:* Yangtze Boatman Chantey

▶ 1) Add brackets to show the phrases. 2) Add a breath mark between the phrases. Chinese Folk Song

Andante

120. E–Z Does It

Andante

121. Mary Ann — *Duet*

Calypso began in early 20th century Caribbean communities where slaves used music to communicate without their master's understanding. Today, the music often features guitar, steel drums, and other percussion instruments accompanying the vocals.

Calypso Song

Moderato

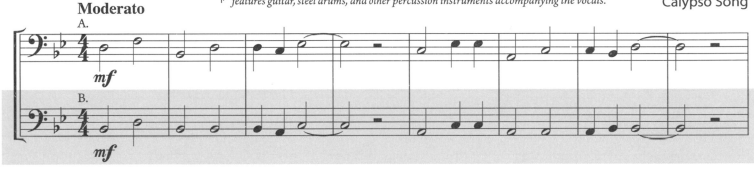

122. Skill Builder: Happy Little Donkey — *Round* ✓TEST

American Folk Song

Andante

123. Excellence in Ear Training

▶ Practice with the recorded accompaniment. Listen in measures 1, 3, 5, and 7. In measures 2, 4, 6, and 8, echo what you heard. Your starting notes are shown.

124. Warm-up: Chop Builders

▶ Are you playing with a fast and steady air stream? Also play this exercise on your mouthpiece alone.

Moderato

mf

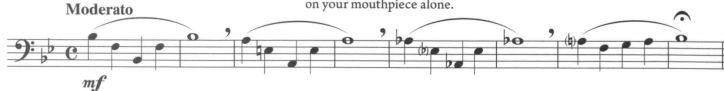

125. Oh Yeah!

▶ Use a focused air stream as you go up to play the C.

Andante

f

126. Skill Builder

Andante

f

ritardando

127. Theme from "The Sleeping Beauty"

▶ Circle the notes changed by the key signature.

In 1891, Tchaikovsky traveled to America for the opening of Carnegie Hall in New York City.

Peter Ilyich Tchaikovsky
(1840–1893)
Russian Composer

Allegro

mp   *f*

rit.   *mp*

128. Amazing Grace ✓ TEST

American Folk Song

Andante

mp   *f*

mp   *rit.*   *p*

129. Baritone/Euphonium Private Lesson

▶ Support each note with plenty of air. Gradually increase the tempo each time you play this exercise.

mf   *f*   *mf*

MASTERING EXCELLENCE: p. 39, #7

Rhythm

syncopation – rhythmic effect that places emphasis on a weak beat

130. A Little Blue

Moderato

The blues developed in the United States during the early 1900s as an outgrowth of African-American spirituals and work songs. Blues melodies are usually 12 measures long.

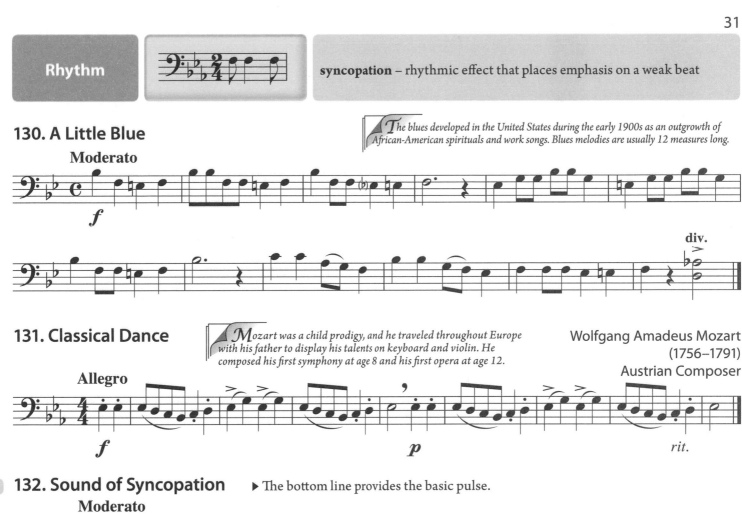

131. Classical Dance

Mozart was a child prodigy, and he traveled throughout Europe with his father to display his talents on keyboard and violin. He composed his first symphony at age 8 and his first opera at age 12.

Wolfgang Amadeus Mozart
(1756–1791)
Austrian Composer

Allegro

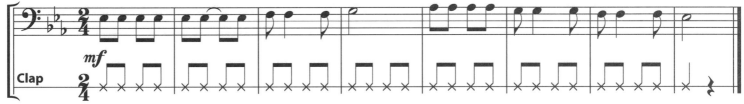

syncopation

132. Sound of Syncopation   ▸ The bottom line provides the basic pulse.

Moderato

Clap

133. Sleeping Princess

Swedish Folk Song

Moderato

134. Skill Builder: Samba-lêlê ✓ TEST

Brazilian Folk Song

Moderato

135. Excellence in Theory

A. Write these tempo marks in the correct blanks: slowest ⟵⟶ fastest

Andante Allegro Moderato   _____   _____   _____

B. Write these dynamic marks in the correct blanks: softest ⟵⟶ loudest

mf   p   f   mp   _____ _____ _____ _____

136. Warm-up: Ye Banks and Braes o' Bonnie Doon — *Duet* Scottish Folk Song

137. Open the Door for Me! ▸ Add brackets to show the phrases. South African Folk Song

138. Shepherd's Hey

Australian-born composer Percy Grainger (1882-1961) is well known for his arrangements of English folk songs and country dances. His 1918 version of **Shepherd's Hey** *for concert band shows Grainger's skills in orchestration, and is part of the band world's standard repertoire.*

English Folk Song

139. The Yellow Rose of Texas American Folk Song

140. Manhattan Beach March ✔ TEST

Sousa played piano, violin, flute, cornet, trombone, and baritone. He is most remembered for his marches, and is known as "The March King."

John Philip Sousa
(1854–1932)
American Composer

ENSEMBLE

The term "military band" was historically used to designate an instrumental ensemble made up of woodwinds, brass, and percussion, much like today's concert band. **Ecossaise for Military Band** was originally written by Beethoven in 1810 for this type of ensemble. The work is a **contradance**, a lively dance-inspired composition in $\frac{2}{4}$. In a contradance, couples faced each other in two lines. It was a Classical Period predecessor to more modern forms such as square dancing.

Solo: A   **Duet:** A + B   **Trio** or **Full Band:** A + B + C

Ecossaise for Military Band

▶ 1st x = first time through. 2nd x = second time through.

Ludwig van Beethoven (1770–1827)
German Composer
arr. Bruce Pearson

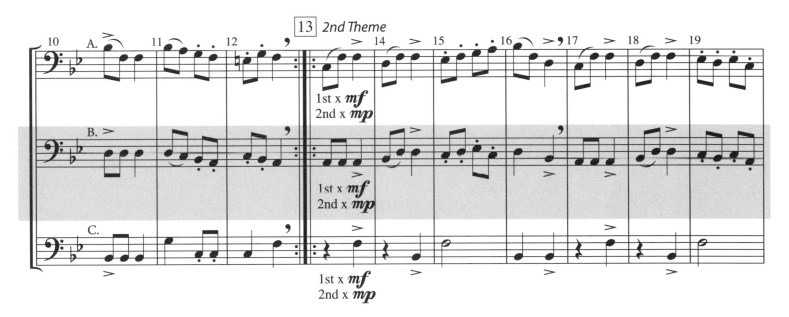

W61BC

Band Pieces

ternary form

See, The Conquering Hero Comes
from "Judas Maccabaeus"

Judas Maccabaeus, composed in 1746, is one of Handel's most famous oratorios. This piece majestically commemorates the title character's victorious return from battle.

George Frideric Handel (1685–1759)
English Composer
arr. Ryan Nowlin

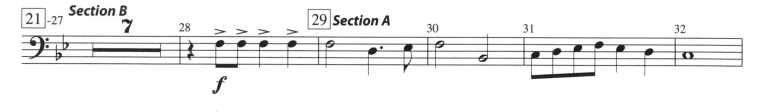

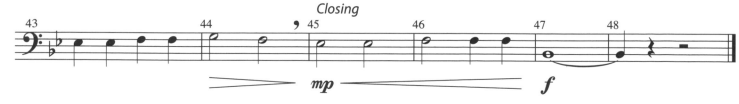

Riverside March

Ryan Nowlin (b. 1978)
American Composer

▶ Notice the key signature changes at 27 and 47.

W61BC

Handel was born in 1685, the same year as Domenico Scarlatti and J.S. Bach!
Handel's Semele is based on Greek mythology, which is unlike most of Handel's works from this time.

Where'er You Walk

From "Semele"
Solo with Piano Accompaniment

George Frideric Handel (1685–1759)
English Composer
arr. Ryan Nowlin

MASTERING EXCELLENCE

1. After page 10, #35

Basic Preparatory Exercise

Advanced Preparatory Exercise

Mastering Excellence

2. After page 16, #60

Basic Preparatory Exercise

Advanced Preparatory Exercise

Mastering Excellence

3. After page 18, #73

Basic Preparatory Exercise

Advanced Preparatory Exercise

Mastering Excellence

4. After page 22, #79

Basic Preparatory Exercise

Advanced Preparatory Exercise

Mastering Excellence

5. After Page 24, #93

Basic Preparatory Exercise

▶ Repeat these exercises using the following fingerings: 0, 2, 1, 12, 23, 13, 123.
Use these as daily warm-ups when you practice. Also play these exercises on your mouthpiece alone.

Advanced Preparatory Exercise

Mastering Excellence

6. After page 26, #106

Basic Preparatory Exercise

Advanced Preparatory Exercise

Mastering Excellence

7. After page 30, #129

Basic Preparatory Exercise

Advanced Preparatory Exercise

Mastering Excellence

GREAT WARM-UPS

Chop Builders

▶ Mix and match exercises 1A, 2A, and 3A in any combination.

1A.

2A.

3A.

1B, 2B, 3B. ▶ Use this line to accompany 1A, 2A, and 3A.

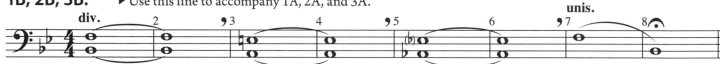

4. Match and Pass That Note

▶ Also play with other articulations:

5. Dynamic Control

B♭ Major Warm-Up (Concert B♭ Major)

1. B♭ Major Scale and Arpeggios

2. B♭ Major Technique Study

▶ Also play with other articulations:

W61BC

3. B♭ Major Balance and Tuning Study

4. B♭ Major Chorale: All Grace and Thanksgiving

Ryan Nowlin (b. 1978)
American Composer

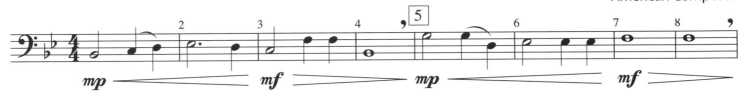

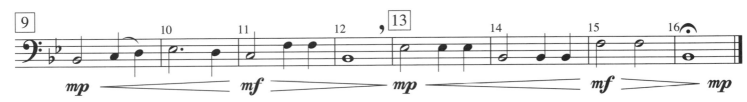

E♭ Major Warm-Up (Concert E♭ Major)

▶ For notes you do not know, refer to the fingering chart.

1. E♭ Major Scale and Arpeggios

2. E♭ Major Technique Study

▶ Also play with other articulations:

3. E♭ Major Balance and Tuning Study

4. E♭ Major Chorale: Make a Joyful Sound

Ryan Nowlin (b. 1978)
American Composer

F Major Warm-Up (Concert F Major)

▶ For notes you do not know, refer to the fingering chart.

1. F Major Scale and Arpeggios

2. F Major Technique Study

▶ Also play with other articulations:

3. F Major Balance and Tuning Study

4. F Major Chorale: Celebration and Honor

Ryan Nowlin (b. 1978)
American Composer

SCALE STUDIES

Theory & Composition — **chromatic scale** – series of 12 ascending or descending half steps

▶ For notes you do not know, refer to the fingering chart.

1. Bb Major Scale, Arpeggios, and Thirds (Concert Bb Major)

2. Eb Major Scale, Arpeggios, and Thirds (Concert Eb Major)

3. F Major Scale, Arpeggios, and Thirds (Concert F Major)

4. Ab Major Scale, Arpeggios, and Thirds (Concert Ab Major)

chromatic
scale

5. Chromatic Scale

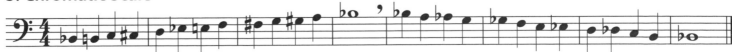

RHYTHM STUDIES

$\frac{4}{4}$ or **C**

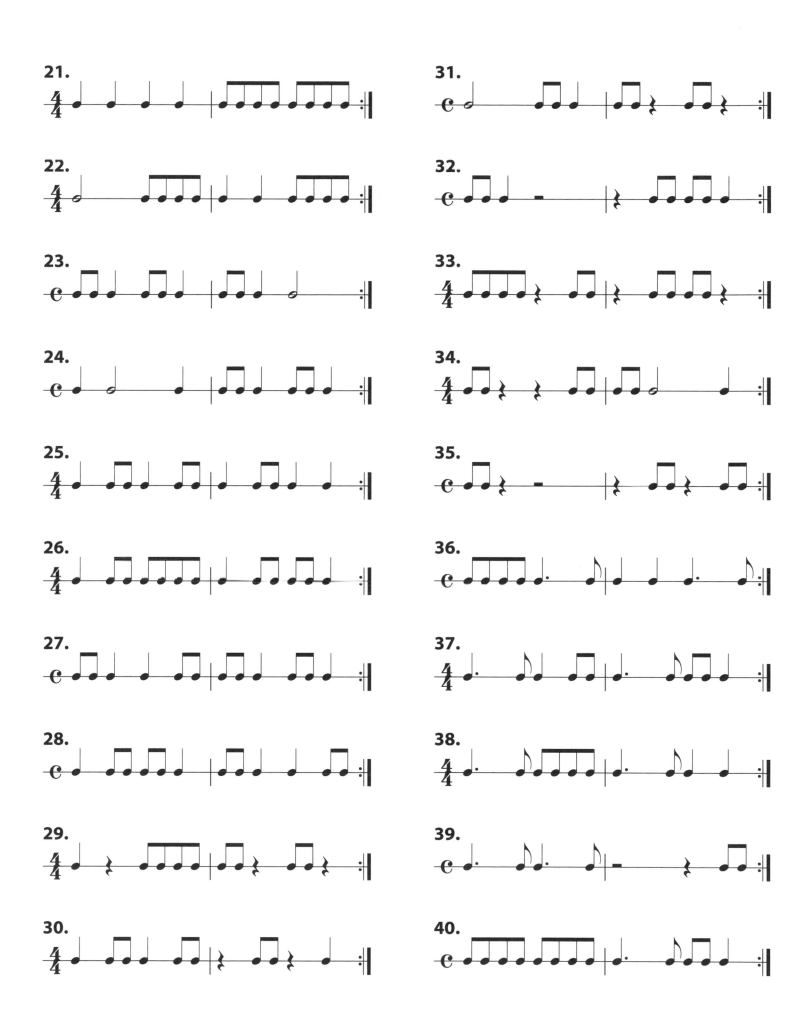

World Map

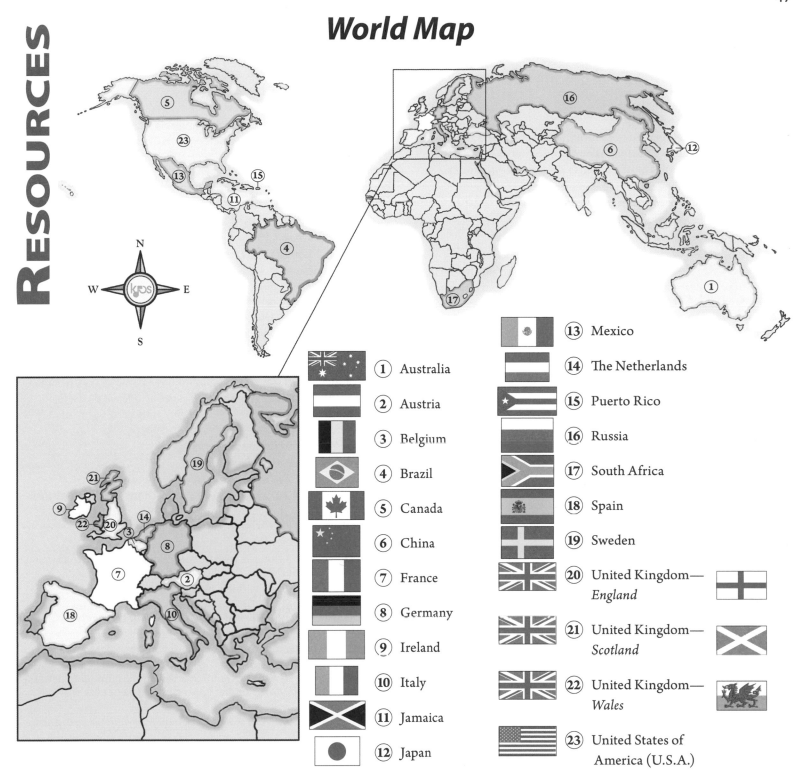

RESOURCES

- 1 Australia
- 2 Austria
- 3 Belgium
- 4 Brazil
- 5 Canada
- 6 China
- 7 France
- 8 Germany
- 9 Ireland
- 10 Italy
- 11 Jamaica
- 12 Japan
- 13 Mexico
- 14 The Netherlands
- 15 Puerto Rico
- 16 Russia
- 17 South Africa
- 18 Spain
- 19 Sweden
- 20 United Kingdom— *England*
- 21 United Kingdom— *Scotland*
- 22 United Kingdom— *Wales*
- 23 United States of America (U.S.A.)

About the Baritone/Euphonium

The baritone shares its history with many other trumpet-like instruments. The early non-valved instruments could only play a few notes and were used for signaling and in ceremonial events. For centuries beginning in Roman times, bass trumpets and horns were commonly used in military and civilian arenas.

Baritones first appeared in the late 1830s, a few years after the invention of valved brass instruments. Baritones were used extensively in military and school bands by 1850, and they were often featured as solo instruments.

In the American Civil War, the band marched at the head of the army, and the bell of the baritone faced backward over the player's left shoulder to be heard by the soldiers. Baritones with bells pointing upward or forward became standard in concert bands, which became more common after the Civil War.

The baritone and the euphonium are very similar. The euphonium is related to the flugelhorn and has a larger bore. The baritone is more closely related to the cornet. Baritones usually have three valves, while euphoniums often have four or even five. Both instruments are played today in concert bands and occasionally in orchestras.

FUN FACTS

- ▶ The word *euphonium* means "good voice" in Greek.
- ▶ The baritone horn can play music written in either treble clef or bass clef.
- ▶ Check out these baritone/euphonium players: Lyndon Baglin, Nicholas Childs, Steven Mead, Adam Frey, and Demondrae Thurman.

Glossary/Index

accent – (p. 18) emphasize the note

accidental – (pp. 4-6) symbol that alters the pitch of a note until the end of the measure

Allegro – (p. 18) fast tempo

anacrusis – (p. 16) see **pick-up**

Andante – (p. 18) walking tempo; slower than **Moderato**

arpeggio – (p. 23) notes of a chord sounded one after another

articulation – (p. 10) type of attack used to play a note or group of notes

bar line – (pp. 4-6) divides the staff into measures

bass clef – (pp. 4-6) locates F on the fourth line

breath mark – (p. 7) take a breath

cautionary accidental – (p. 24) see **courtesy accidental**

chord – (p. 20) two or more notes sounded at the same time

chromatic scale – (p. 43) scale of 12 ascending or descending half steps

closing – (p. 20) last measures of a composition, often containing new material added to give a feeling of finality

common time – (p. 9) means the same as ₄⁄₄

composition – (p. 9) creation of music that can be performed later, usually from written notation

courtesy accidental – (p. 24) reminder that the bar line has canceled an accidental

crescendo – (p. 22) gradually louder

Da Capo al Fine (**D.C. al Fine**) – (p. 26) go back to the beginning of the piece and play or sing until the *Fine*

decrescendo – (p. 22) gradually softer

Divisi (**div.**) – (p. 22) some performers play or sing the top notes while others play or sing the bottom notes

dominant – (p. 20) fifth note of a scale; chord built on the fifth note of a scale

duet – (p. 7) piece of music featuring two different parts played or sung together

dynamics – (p. 17) softness or loudness of a piece of music

embouchure – (p. 3) mouth formation used to play an instrument

F clef – (pp. 4-6) see **bass clef**

fermata – (p. 12) hold a note or rest longer than its usual value

final double bar line – (pp. 4-6) marks the end of the music

1st and 2nd endings – (p. 12) play or sing the 1st ending the first time through, repeat, skip the 1st ending, and play or sing the 2nd ending

flat – (pp. 4-6) lowers the pitch of a note one half step

forte (*f*) – (p. 17) loud

half step – (pp. 4-6) smallest interval used in Western music

harmony – (p. 7) two or more notes played or sung at the same time

improvisation – (p. 15) spontaneous composition of music through playing or singing

interval – (pp. 4-6) distance between two pitches

introduction – (p. 12) opening passage of a piece of music

key signature – (p. 11) sharps or flats placed after a clef

ledger line – (pp. 4-6) short line used for notes above or below the staff

long rest – (p. 20) rest for the number of measures indicated

Maestoso – (p. 27) majestically

major scale – (p. 23) series of whole (w) and half (h) steps in the following pattern: wwhwwwh

measure – (pp. 4-6) area between two bar lines

mezzo forte (*mf*) – (p. 18) medium loud

mezzo piano (*mp*) – (p. 18) medium soft

Moderato – (p. 18) medium tempo

multiple-measure rest – (p. 20) see **long rest**

music alphabet – (pp. 4-6) first seven letters of the alphabet; these note names are assigned to the lines and spaces of the staff

natural – (p. 22) cancels a flat or sharp

one-measure repeat sign – (p. 10) play or sing the previous measure again

orchestration – (p. 23) choice of instruments used to play the music

phrase – (p. 9) musical sentence, often 4 or 8 measures long

piano (*p*) – (p. 17) soft

pick-up – (p. 16) music that comes before the first full measure of a piece

rehearsal number – (p. 12) find important places in the music using these markers

repeat sign – (p. 9) play or sing the music again

ritardando (*ritard.* or *rit.*) – (p. 30) gradually slow the tempo

round – (p. 9) song in which the same part is played or sung by two or more groups starting at different times

sharp – (p. 24) raises the pitch of a note one half step

sight-reading – (p. 7) playing or singing a piece of music for the first time

slur – (p. 10) articulation that connects notes of *different* pitches; indicates a very smooth sound

Soli – (p. 9) a small group or section plays or sings

Solo – (p. 9) only one person plays or sings

staccato – (p. 25) shorten the note

staff – (pp. 4-6) 5 lines and 4 spaces for writing music

subdominant – (p. 20) fourth note of a scale; chord built on the fourth note of a scale

syncopation – (p. 31) rhythmic effect that places emphasis on a weak beat

tempo – (p. 18) speed of a piece of music

ternary form – (p. 34) music with three sections: Section A, followed by a contrasting Section B, then Section A again

theme – (p. 12) a melody within a piece of music

theme and variation – (p. 16) type of composition that begins with a main melody (**theme**) and continues with different versions (**variations**) of the main melody

tie – (p. 11) marking that connects notes of the *same* pitch to make one longer note

time signature – (pp. 4-6) top number tells you the number of counts per measure; bottom number tells you the type of note that gets one count

tonic – (p. 20) first note of a scale; chord built on the first note of a scale

trio (ensemble) – (p. 12) piece of music featuring three different parts played or sung together

trio (march) – (p. 34) third theme in a march, typically a contrasting section

Tutti – (p. 9) everyone plays or sings

unisono (**unis.**) – (p. 22) everyone plays or sings the same notes

variation – (p. 16) see **theme and variation**

whole step – (p. 23) interval consisting of two half steps

Timeline

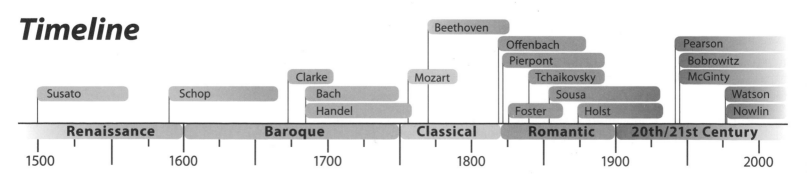